To:
_____

From:
_____

You're Invited
to Begin Your Easter at:
_____

EASTER

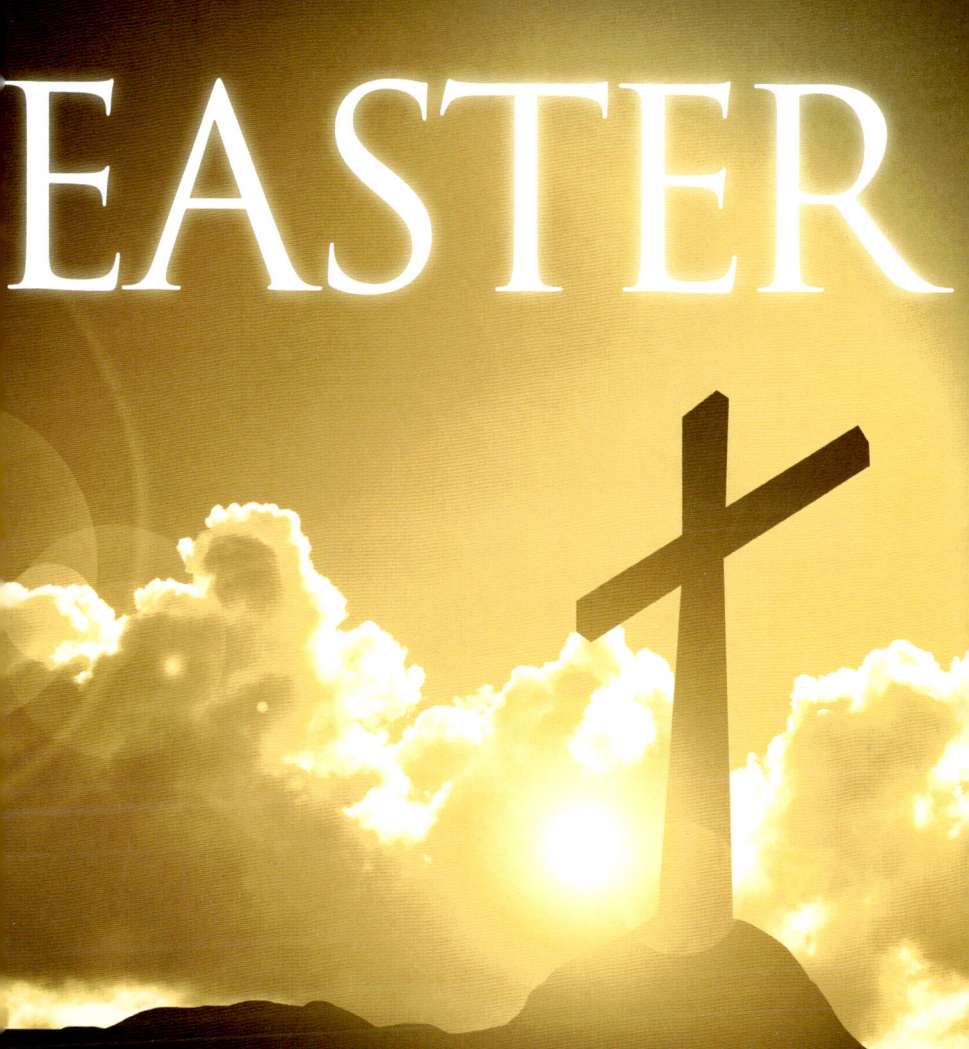

A Fresh Retelling of the Resurrection of Jesus

Written by Paul Langham

OUTREACH®

The Easter Story: A Fresh Retelling of the Resurrection of Jesus
Text Copyright © 2013 by Paul Langham
Cover Copyright © 2013 by Outreach
Published under license from Kingsley Books, Inc., Nashville, Tennessee

Some of the selections in this book based on the gospel of Matthew are adapted from *Who?* by Paul Langham and published with permission of the British and Foreign Bible Society www.biblesociety.org.uk

All rights reserved. No part of this book may be reproduced in any form or by any electronic or mechanical means, including information storage and retrieval systems, photocopy, recording, scanning or other, without permission in writing from the publisher, except by a reviewer who may quote brief passages in a review.

All Scripture quotations, unless otherwise indicated, are taken from the HOLY BIBLE, NEW INTERNATIONAL VERSION®, NIV®, Copyright © 1973, 1978, 1984, 2011 by Biblica. Used by permission of Zondervan Publishing House. All rights reserved worldwide.

Published by Outreach, Inc., Colorado Springs, CO 80919

www.outreach.com

ISBN: 978-1-9355-4187-5

Written by: Paul Langham
Cover Design: Tim Downs
Interior Design: Stephanie Larson

Printed in the United States of America

Before You Begin...

Two thousand years ago there lived a man named Jesus—whose life, teachings, death, and resurrection changed the course of human history. Four of His closest friends wrote accounts of His life, called gospels, which simply means "good news." All of them devoted a large portion of their writings to what happened in the last week of Jesus' life.

But the story really begins hundreds of years before Jesus was born. God's messengers promised that God would send a Savior to our world. They predicted the suffering Jesus willingly endured to make it possible for us to know peace with God. One of the clearest of these descriptions of the life and death of Jesus was written by the prophet Isaiah:

> People could hardly bear to look at Him, He was so bruised and broken—He looked barely human. But entire peoples will one day marvel at Him; even kings will stand speechless before Him.
>
> He grew like a fragile flower taking root in dry ground. He was no sight for sore eyes; nothing about Him attracted admiring glances. If people paid Him any heed at all, it was only to look down their noses at Him and turn their backs. He was no stranger to sorrow and pain.
>
> But He shouldered all our wrongdoing and labored under the weight of our grief. We thought God had it in for Him, so harshly was He punished. But He was nailed because of our shortcomings; He was crushed under the weight of our sins. The price of our peace was inflicted on His body, and His wounds have healed us.

You and me—we're like sheep, straying from the path, each of us striking blindly out on our own, not even knowing we're lost. And God has punished Him for our acts of rebellion.

He went through hell for us. Yet like a lamb about to be butchered, He didn't utter so much as a single bleat of protest. Arrested and tried, His so-called judge ordered, "Take Him down." No chance of seeing out His years; no hope of family or future. His life was snuffed out, his deathblow dealt by our sins. He was lumped with all the riffraff, even though He had not harmed a soul and had never spoken a deceitful word in His life.

It was God's will that He should suffer and be crushed. For it was God's ancient plan that His blood would wash away the stains of our guilt. Because of His faithfulness, God will give Him life again, and He will see the fruit of His appalling suffering. Because of His obedience, He will have many children—all those who trust in His saving death— and He will be given glory and honor. He poured out His life like water, and He carried the sins of countless millions.
based on selections from Isaiah 53

What follows in this booklet is the story of Jesus' death and resurrection that His friends recorded in the gospels, but written as it might sound if the story were written today. And of course it is only part of the story. So after you have read this little booklet, we encourage you to read the entire life of Jesus in one of the many modern versions of the Bible. You will find the gospels at the beginning of the section called the New Testament.

THE EASTER STORY: A FRESH RETELLING OF THE RESURRECTION OF JESUS

Jesus' friends wrote their accounts to help people understand and believe that Jesus' death and resurrection makes it possible for everyone to be forgiven for the all the things they have done wrong, to live at peace with God, and to have the assurance of eternal life. We pray this booklet will introduce you to the God who loves you so much that He was willing to come and die to prove it.

EASTER

A Fresh Retelling of the Resurrection of Jesus

Jesus, Healer and Teacher

Jesus traveled from town to town, telling everyone the good news of God's invitation to enter His kingdom, and backing up His teaching by healing every sickness and disease. The crowds flocked to Him, and His heart broke for them. They were so lost and helpless, like sheep without a shepherd to lead them and keep them safe.

The news reached John the Baptist, who sent two of his own followers to ask Jesus whether He was indeed the Savior whom God had promised. Jesus sent them back to John, saying, "Go and tell John what you've seen and heard. Those who were once blind gaze around them, and those who were once lame skip with joy, the skin of lepers glows with health, those who were once deaf drink in the sound of birdsong, the dead breathe again, and those who know their need of God's love hear the good news of His kingdom."

After this, one of the religious leaders invited Jesus to supper. He was surprised when Jesus didn't bother with the rules about ceremonial washing before eating.

Reading his mind, Jesus said, "What's the point of washing the outside of a bowl if you leave the inside filthy? In the same way, ceremonial washing is utterly pointless if a person's inner life is corrupt. How crazy to imagine that God, who made you and knows your inner life, would be fooled for a moment … Don't you religious leaders just love the best seats in the synagogue? You lap it up when the ordinary people bow and scrape to you! You'd never know it to look at you, yet behind all your fancy show, you reek of decay and corruption. You're like unmarked graves!"

Well, that was some supper party! From that time on, Jesus was a marked man. The religious leaders set their faces in opposition to Him and besieged Him with questions and challenges, hoping to find some way of tripping Him up.

The ordinary people were divided in their opinions. Some considered Him a good man, others, a charlatan. But whatever their views, they kept them quiet—no one dared let the religious leaders overhear them talking about Jesus. The word was out that anyone who acknowledged Jesus was the Savior would be banned from worshipping in any synagogue.
based on Matthew 9:35–36; Luke 7:18–22, 11:37–54; John 7:12–13, 9:22

Passover in Jerusalem

It was almost time for one of the great Jewish feasts, called the Passover, a time when the Jews remembered how God led their ancestors out from Egypt in a great escape. The religious leaders were racking their brains for a way to get rid of Jesus, because they were jealous and could see He threatened their authority and hold over the people.

The crowds in Jerusalem—both those who lived there and those who had come in from far and wide for the feast—kept looking for Jesus. Everyone speculated whether He would show up or not. Anyone who saw Him was supposed to be report it to the religious leaders immediately.

On His way to Jerusalem with His followers, Jesus caught a few quiet moments alone with them. "I want you to be clear about what lies ahead," He told them. "In Jerusalem, I'll be betrayed to the religious authorities. They'll condemn me and arrange for the Romans to crucify me. But three days later, I'll be raised to life again."
based on Luke 22:1–2, John 11:55–57, Matthew 20:17–19

The King Is Coming!

Their approach to Jerusalem brought Jesus and His followers to two small villages just outside the city, near the Mount of Olives. Jesus sent two of His disciples into one of the villages, with instructions to bring Him a donkey and to promise to return it to the owner shortly. Bringing it to Jesus, they made a saddle of their cloaks, and so Jesus entered the capital city riding on a donkey. There was a carnival atmosphere among His followers—some

threw their cloaks on the road in front of Him; others cut down palm branches. The sound of cheering rose above the clamor, as people grew ever more excited about what would happen when Jesus entered Jerusalem. "Hosanna!" they shouted. "Hosanna to the great king. Bring back the glory days of King David!" But Jesus didn't stay in the city long that first day. He went into the temple, taking careful note of all He saw there, and then left to spend the night in a nearby village called Bethany.
based on Mark 11:1–11

Trouble at the Temple

Entering the temple, Jesus found the outer courtyard cluttered with traders making a fast profit from those coming to worship, charging exorbitant rates to change money or for the small birds needed for the temple sacrifices. Jesus drove them out, overturning their tables, their coins scattering everywhere. "The holy writings call God's temple a house of prayer, but you've turned it into a place of daylight robbery," Jesus said.

People flocked to Jesus at the temple, and He healed those who were blind and disabled. Children ran around, shouting, "Hosanna! Praise the son of the great king David!" This made the religious authorities angry.

Those who had witnessed Lazarus rising from the dead couldn't keep quiet about what they had seen, and this further swelled the crowds who came to see the one who had performed such an amazing miracle. The religious leaders were at a loss to know what to do. It seemed to them that the whole world had gone mad about Jesus.

Judas, one of the Twelve, went to the religious authorities and asked, "What will you give me to betray Jesus?" He settled for thirty pieces of silver and waited for his opportunity.
based on Matthew 21:12–15, John 12:17–19, Matthew 26:14–16

THE EASTER STORY: A FRESH RETELLING OF THE RESURRECTION OF JESUS

One Last Meal

That evening, Jesus gathered with His followers to eat the Passover supper. The stage was set. The enemy had already prompted Judas to betray Jesus, who knew that everything was working out according to God's plan. It wouldn't be long now until His stay on earth was over and He would rejoin His Father in heaven. Knowing full well that this was His last opportunity to be with them, Jesus found a very special way to show just how much He loved them all and to give them an example to follow.

As supper was being served, Jesus wrapped a towel round His waist, fetched a bowl of water, and knelt down. One by one, He began to wash and dry His disciples' feet. Peter tried to stop Him, but Jesus said, "I know this doesn't make sense to you right now, but it won't be long before you will understand. I'm giving you a pattern of how things are to be among my followers. You are happy to call me Lord and Teacher—that's what I am. Well, now you see that I'm happy to be your servant too. Don't forget this lesson—treat each other as I have treated you. If you live this way, you will always know God's blessing and favor."

Jesus said, "One of you sharing this meal is about to betray me. Everything prophesied about me long ago is about to unfold. As for the traitor, it would have been better for him never to have been born."

His followers were horrified, and each one in turn asked: "Do you mean me?" Judas had the nerve to ask whether he was the one. Jesus said simply, "Yes, you are."
based on John 13:1–17, Matthew 26:21–25

"My Body Will Be Broken for You"

During the meal, Jesus said, "I have been looking forward to this moment for a long time. It will be the last time I share a Passover meal or drink wine with you until after my resurrection." Then He took a piece of bread and gave thanks to God. As He broke it slowly into pieces, He said, "My body will be broken for you, just like this piece of bread. Eat it to remember me."

At the end of the meal, He took a cup of wine and said, "This marks God's new promise, written in my blood, which will soon be poured out for you like this wine. But a traitor's hand is here on the table. My destiny will unfold according to God's plan, but pity the man who betrays me." At this, they all began to whisper among themselves as to who it could possibly be.

Turning to Peter, Jesus sighed, "Oh Peter, Peter, the enemy has you in his sights and is going to test you severely. I've prayed for strength for you, that your faith may not fail. When you're back on course, strengthen the others."

Peter said, "I'm ready for anything the enemy can throw at me, even if it means prison or death."

"Peter, Peter," said Jesus, "before dawn comes, you will deny all knowledge of me, not just once, but three times."

"Never," Peter swore. "I'd sooner die than abandon you." And they all said the same.

Jesus' talk of death distressed His disciples deeply, so He said to them, "Don't let your hearts be heavy. You've always trusted in God, haven't you? Well then, now trust me too … Don't think I'm leaving you forever. All I'm really doing is going to My Father's house to get your rooms ready. I'll come back for you and take you back home with me. And you know the way to where I am going."

Thomas spoke for all the disciples. "We haven't a clue where you're going. How will we know the right way?"

Jesus answered, "I am the way and the truth and the life. I am the only way to the Father. To know me is to know Him. If you look at me, you're seeing the Father himself."

They sang a hymn together and went out into the night, heading for the Mount of Olives.
based on Luke 22:14–23, 31–33; Matthew 26:35; John 14:1–7; Mark 14:26

Betrayed by a Kiss

Leading them all into a garden called Gethsemane, Jesus said, "Wait here. I need to pray alone for a while." He took Peter, James, and John deeper into the garden, where He became visibly distressed and said to them, "I feel as though I'm being crushed with a great sadness. It's enough to finish me. Stay here and watch with me."

A few steps later, He fell down and called out, "Father, if there's any way out of this, please rescue me. But I'm ready to do whatever you ask of me."

Returning to His followers, He found them all asleep. Waking Peter, He asked, "Is one hour too much to ask of you? Stay awake, and ask God for strength to resist the temptation you are going to face. I know you want to do the right thing, but your spirit is weak."

Jesus returned to prayer: "Father, if there is no other way, you know I'm ready to go through with it. I'm yours to command." The disciples had fallen asleep again, so He left them for a third time, continuing to ask His Father for escape but promising to obey Him, whatever the outcome.

Jesus then woke His followers. "Are you still asleep? Well, you have had all the rest you are going to get. On your feet! The time has come. See! The traitor approaches."

As Jesus spoke, Judas appeared with an armed mob sent by the religious authorities. As bold as brass, he walked straight up to Jesus. "Teacher," he said, and kissed Him. He had told the mob, "That will be the one you need to arrest."

"My friend," Jesus said, "no need for pretense; just do what you have come to do." As the mob seized Jesus, one of His followers drew a sword and slashed at the high priest's servant, cutting off his ear.

"That's enough!" Jesus said, touching the servant and healing his ear. "Violence never brings life, only death. If I wanted to use force, I could ask My Father to summon battalions of angels to my side. But everything must take its course, just as it was written long ago."

At this, all Jesus' followers turned and ran, leaving Him alone.
based on Matthew 26:36–56, Luke 22:51

Jesus before the High Priest

The mob dragged Jesus to the home of Caiaphas, the high priest, where the religious leaders had assembled. Peter followed, slipping in and out of the shadows, and managed to get into the courtyard of the house.

The tribunal was looking for any excuse to condemn Jesus to death, but even though they had arranged for "witnesses" to tell lies about Jesus, none of their stories agreed. Finally, two men claimed, "He boasted about destroying the temple and rebuilding it in three days!"

Caiaphas jumped up. "What do you say to that?" he demanded. But Jesus remained silent, until the high priest asked Him outright, "You are under oath, so tell us the truth. Are you the Messiah, the Son of God?"

"Yes, I am," Jesus replied, "and one day you will see me at God's right hand, and returning to earth on the clouds."

"Blasphemy!" Caiaphas shouted, tearing at his robes in fury. "What more evidence do we need?"

"He must die!" the leaders shouted, and began to spit at Him and hit Him with their fists.

Outside in the courtyard, a servant girl spotted Peter. "You are one of Jesus' followers, aren't you?"

"I have no idea what you're talking about," Peter said, loud enough for all to hear, and moved away.

Another girl recognized him. "Look," she said. "He was with Jesus."

"You have it all wrong," Peter swore. "I have never even met the man."

A little later, they all challenged Peter. "Come on," they said. "Your northern accent gives you away as one of Jesus' men."

Peter began to swear and curse. "How many times do I have to tell you, I don't know Him!" At that very moment, a cock crowed in the chill of the new dawn. Peter remembered what Jesus had said, and running outside, he broke down and wept uncontrollably.
based on Matthew 26:57–75

A Kangaroo Court

Early that morning, the religious authorities agreed that Jesus must die. So they cuffed Him and handed Him over to the Roman governor, a man called Pilate.

When Judas realized Jesus had been condemned to death, he was filled with remorse and tried to hand his blood money back. "I have done a terrible wrong," he said. "I've betrayed an innocent man."

"That's your problem," they replied, refusing to take it. "It has nothing to do with us." So Judas flung the money into the temple, then went out to a field and hanged himself.

Meanwhile, Pilate was questioning Jesus. "Are you the king of the Jews?"

"I am," Jesus replied.

When the chief priests outlined their charges against Him, however, Jesus made no reply. "Do you hear what they are saying?" Pilate asked, but to his amazement, Jesus would say no more.

When Pilate told the religious leaders that he could find no basis for any of their claims, they pressed on with their accusations. "He's a rabble-rouser," they said. "He has been whipping up the people all the way from Galilee to here."
based on Matthew 27:1–5, 11–14; Luke 23:4–5

THE EASTER STORY: A FRESH RETELLING OF THE RESURRECTION OF JESUS

"Release Barabbas: Crucify Jesus"

Pilate was no fool; he could see through the trumped-up charges against Jesus to the envy that lay behind them. His politician's mind thought it saw a way out. Pilate had established a popular Passover tradition of allowing the crowds to choose one prisoner to be set free. He called out to the festival crowds, "It's time to choose a prisoner! You can have Jesus, the one you call Messiah, or you can have Barabbas." Barabbas was a real thug, and Pilate was sure they would choose to set Jesus free.

But the religious authorities stirred up the crowd to demand Barabbas. "Give us Barabbas!" they shouted.

"What about Jesus, then?" asked Pilate. "What shall I do with Him?"

"Kill Him!" they bellowed.

"Why? What's His crime?" Pilate replied. But there was no persuading them.

"Crucify Him!" they yelled, over and over again. Pilate recognized trouble when he saw it. He knew when to cut his losses. So he washed his hands in front of the crowd. "I'm not responsible for what you do to this man," he said.

"Let it be on our own heads!" people shouted.

So Pilate had Jesus whipped and let them take Him away to be crucified.
based on Matthew 27:15–26

JESUS IS CRUCIFIED

The soldiers took Jesus into the palace. They draped a purple cloak around His shoulders, twisted some thorn branches into a crude crown, and stuck it on His head. They knelt before Him in mock homage, beat Him about the head with a staff, and spat at Him again and again. "Hail, man who would be king!" they shouted, their harsh voices dripping with sarcasm. Then they pulled off the purple robe, dressed Jesus in His own clothes, and led Him away to be executed.

On the way, the soldiers forced a man named Simon, coming into the city for the festival, to carry Jesus' cross. At "Skull Place" they offered Jesus wine to dull the pain, but He refused. Then they stretched Him out on the cross and drove nails through His feet and wrists. Lifting Him up, they dropped the cross into its socket and sat down. As they waited for Jesus to die, they played dice for His clothes.

As was custom, they fixed a sign to the cross above His head detailing His crime: "Here hangs Jesus, king of the Jews." People in the crowd joined the religious elite in hurling insults at Jesus. "You boasted you could tear down the temple and raise it again in three days. So what's your problem? If you really were the Son of God, you would surely be able to save yourself. After all, you claimed the power to save others. Call yourself king of the Jews? Come on, then, prove it! Or get God to rescue you. Surely He would do that for His Son!"

At noon, darkness fell over the whole region. At about three in the afternoon, Jesus cried out in a loud voice, "My God, my God, why have you abandoned me?" Some of the bystanders thought

He had called out to Elijah. One of them put a sponge into wine vinegar and stuck it on a stick for Jesus to drink. "Now let's leave Him alone and see whether Elijah comes to save Him." With a loud cry, Jesus let out His final breath.

When Jesus died, the curtain that hung in front of the most holy place in the temple split right down the middle from top to bottom. The soldier on guard over the crucifixion, seeing how Jesus died, said, "Without doubt this man was God's own Son."

A group of women, followers of Jesus, stood forlornly at a distance, watching everything that happened.
based on Mark 15:16–20, Matthew 27:32–44, Mark 15:33–41

Buried in a Rock Tomb

It was the Roman practice to break the legs of those being crucified, as this speeded death and ensured the victims had not simply fainted. But when the soldiers came to Jesus, He was clearly dead so they did not bother. Just to be sure, however, one of them stuck a spear into His side, and a mixture of blood and water flowed from the wound.

Because Jesus had been executed on the day before the Jewish day of rest, Jewish law required that His body be buried before sunset. Toward evening, Joseph of Arimathea, a prominent member of the Jewish council, a man who was searching for the kingdom of God, summoned up his courage and went to ask Pilate for Jesus' body. Pilate was surprised that He was already dead. So he double-checked with the soldiers who had crucified Jesus. Then, satisfied that Jesus was truly dead, Pilate gave Joseph permission to remove the body. Joseph bought a roll of linen and wrapped Jesus' body. Then he placed the body into a tomb cut into rock, and rolled a stone over the entrance. Some of the women who had witnessed Jesus' death noted where Jesus was buried.

The next day, the religious authorities sought an audience with Pilate. "Before He died, this con man bluffed that He would rise again after three days. So will you have the tomb sealed and guarded, at least until tomorrow? Otherwise, His followers might steal the body in order to pretend He had indeed come back to life. Imagine the trouble that could stir up."

"Take some of my troops to stand guard duty," Pilate said. "And make the tomb as secure as a bank vault." So they sealed the stone at the mouth of the tomb and set a guard outside.
based on John 19:32–37, Mark 15:42–47, Matthew 27:62–66

"He Isn't Here"

At dawn on the first day of the week, as two women who were Jesus' followers traveled toward the tomb, an earthquake shook the ground. An angel, bright as lightning, pushed away the stone that covered the tomb and sat on it. The terrified guards looked as if they were dead.

"There's no need to be afraid," the angel told the women when they arrived. "You have come looking for Jesus, but He is not here anymore. He's alive, just as He promised. Look, you can see where His body lay. Then go and tell the others He will be waiting for them in Galilee."

As the women rushed off, they ran into Jesus himself. Falling to the ground, they clung to His feet and worshipped Him. "Don't be scared. Go and tell the others I will see them back in Galilee."

Some of the guards went and reported what had happened. The religious leaders bribed the soldiers not to breathe a word to anyone. "Tell everyone that His followers came and stole the body while you were asleep," they said. "Stick to your story. If Pilate gets wind of it, we'll square it all with him." So the soldiers pocketed the money and did as they were told. And their story is still making the rounds today.

When the women reached the place where Jesus' followers were staying, they announced what they had seen and heard. But for most, it seemed too crazy to be true. How could they take it in? Peter and John, however, got up and ran to the tomb. Peter arrived first, and stooping to peer inside, he saw the linen wrappings lying by themselves. Then he left, trying to figure it all out.
based on Matthew 28:1–15, Luke 24:9–12

THE EASTER STORY: A FRESH RETELLING OF THE RESURRECTION OF JESUS

Encounters with Jesus

Later that day, two of Jesus' followers trudged sadly back to their home village, Emmaus, a few miles outside Jerusalem. As they mulled over everything that had happened in the last few days, Jesus joined them and walked along with them. They didn't realize it was Him—who expects to see a dead man?

He asked them, "What are you talking about?" They were the very picture of dejection, all slumped shoulders and long faces. One of them, Cleopas, said, "What planet have you been on these last few days? You must be about the only person alive who doesn't know what's been going on."

"What *has* been going on?" asked Jesus.

"They've killed Jesus of Nazareth, that's what! Oh, what a man—the things He said; the things He did! No one could have had the power He had unless God sent Him. And what did our so-called religious leaders do with Him? They handed Him over to the Romans for crucifixion, that's what. And we had pinned all our hopes on Him. We really believed He was going to save the whole nation. All this happened three days ago, and now some of our women are telling stories of angels at His tomb and that He has risen from the dead! Some of the men went to check it out—they found the tomb empty all right, no sign of Him."

Jesus said, "Can't you put two and two together? How can you be so slow! It's all there in the ancient prophecies. God's messengers of old set it all down for you, if only you could see." So Jesus began to point out every reference in the Jewish texts that had been written about himself.

When the disciples reached the outskirts of their village, it was already dusk, so they persuaded their companion to spend the night. Once supper had been served, Jesus took some bread, gave thanks to God, broke it, and began to hand it to them. At once, they knew who He was, and in that moment, He vanished.

"No wonder we felt so fired up as He talked to us on the road!" they said. Leaving their meal, they set out to return to Jerusalem. Bursting into the room where Jesus' followers were gathered, they were just in time to hear that Jesus had appeared to Peter too.
based on Luke 24:13–35

Jesus Suddenly Appeared

While they were swapping stories, Jesus suddenly appeared in the midst of them, and said, "Peace be with you." His followers thought He was a ghost. "Why the fear? Why the doubts?" Jesus said. "See my hands and feet? Here are the holes left by the nails. It's really me! Touch me if you like; what ghost was ever made of flesh and bone?" Still they couldn't accept the truth, so He asked for some food and ate a piece of cooked fish before their very eyes.

"Surely you remember all I taught you?" Jesus said. "Everything that has happened to me was carefully predicted in advance by God's messengers of old. I was always going to be put to death, and I was always going to rise from the dead on the third day. It's all there in the holy writings—right under your noses! And now the good news of God's love and forgiveness for all who genuinely want a new start will flow out from Jerusalem to the four corners of the earth. You are my witnesses. Soon I will send you the

power you need, just as Father God has promised. But you must stay in the city until then."
based on Luke 24:36–49

"Throw Away Your Doubts"

One of Jesus' followers, Thomas, wasn't there when Jesus appeared. When the others told him they had seen Jesus, he simply couldn't accept it. "Unless I have proof," he said, "unless I actually feel His wounds, there is no way I'm believing that."

A week later, Jesus' followers gathered again in the same house, and this time Thomas was with them. The doors were locked, there was no way in, yet suddenly Jesus appeared. Turning to Thomas, He said, "Here are my wounds, here's your proof. Touch, throw away your doubts, and believe."

"From this day forward," Thomas said, "I own you as my Lord and my God!"

"You have believed because you were given proof," Jesus replied, "Blessed are those who will believe without proof, on faith alone."

Later, Jesus' eleven remaining followers went to Galilee to meet Jesus there. They worshipped Him, although some still held on to doubts. "I have been given absolute authority," Jesus said. "So now I commission you: go to the whole world, calling people everywhere to follow me. Baptize them in the name of the Father, the Son, and the Holy Spirit, and train them to obey my teaching. Don't worry. You will never be alone. I'll be with you every step of the way, to the very end of time."
based on John 20:24–29, Matthew 28:16–20

Jesus Returns to The Father

Jesus took His followers back out to Bethany one last time. Lifting His hands in farewell and blessing them, He was taken from their sight, and they knew that He had returned to be with the Father in heaven. They worshipped Him and returned to Jerusalem, hearts bursting with joy. Day by day they were found in the temple, praising God.

There isn't space here to record all the miracles and signs Jesus did in our presence. In fact, all the books in the world couldn't hold it all. But we can all testify to the truth of what is written here. And this is written that you may believe that Jesus is the Savior, the Son of God. If you trust Him for forgiveness, you will find life in all its fullness.
based on Luke 24:50–53; John 20:30–31, 21:25

THE EASTER STORY: A FRESH RETELLING OF THE RESURRECTION OF JESUS

WHAT NEXT?

After reading this booklet, if you would like to join the millions of people around the world today who seek to follow Jesus Christ, we invite you to pray the prayer on this page. Or you could use your own words. Prayer is not particularly difficult—it's just like talking to a friend. All you need to do is acknowledge your own wrongdoing, express your belief that Jesus' death and resurrection sets you free from your sins—not just for the rest of this life but for the whole of eternity—and ask God to come into your life by the power of His Holy Spirit.

> Dear God,
> Thank You for showing me the truth about Jesus.
> I believe that You created everything and love every person who has ever lived, including me.
> I acknowledge that I have sinned, and I am sorry for living my life apart from You.
> I believe that You sent Your Son, Jesus Christ, to show how much You love me. Jesus died for me on the cross. I believe that His death dealt once and for all with all the things I have ever done wrong or even will do in the future. I believe He rose from the dead and that His death and resurrection provide new life for me now and forever.
> I choose today to trust Jesus as my Savior and Lord, and I ask You to give me Your Holy Spirit to help me live as His follower for the rest of my life.
> Please come into my life, save me, and give me the gift of eternal life. In the name of Jesus I pray.
> Amen.

THE EASTER STORY: A FRESH RETELLING OF THE RESURRECTION OF JESUS

If you have prayed this prayer, we want to welcome you to the family of God. We encourage you to read your Bible regularly and start talking to God day by day, for He is now your heavenly Father and Jesus is your Lord and Savior. We hope that you become part of a local church family that will help you grow in your faith, because it's much harder to follow Jesus on your own and not nearly as much fun!

> "Yet to all who did receive him, to those who believed in his name, he gave the right to become children of God."
>
> John 1:12

THE EASTER STORY: A FRESH RETELLING OF THE RESURRECTION OF JESUS